Happy time unit:

How to Overcome Distraction, Spend More Time on What Matters, and Reduce Stress.

By

Andrew C. Johnson

Table of contents

Introduction

What is the use of time?

You only get 24 hours every day, and although there are lots of methods to squeeze more out of the time you have, there isn't a way to obtain more of the stuff. But no need to worry—there are lots of ways to make the most of your time.

How to Make the Most of Your Time
Here are 7 easy and efficient methods to spend your time better:

1. Slow Down
Slowing down to get more out of your time may sound paradoxical, but when you truly slow down, you will discover that what you do becomes a lot more significant.

Imagine for a second that you're traveling through a lovely forest. Your music is playing a new song, you're chatting to a buddy in the passenger's seat, and before you know it—whoosh—you drove straight through the forest, and it was as if you weren't there at all.

Now imagine that instead of driving in a noisy car, you're walking through the same forest. Summer is transforming into autumn, and as the leaves fall around you, you take in a deep intake of warm, October air.

Your stroll is 10 times more significant since you slowed down. You were able to appreciate the sights, sounds, and fragrances around you, and what you were doing became much more significant. Slowing down brings meaning to how you spend your time, whether you're walking through a forest, spending time with a loved one, playing an instrument, or even working on a report at work.

2. Structure Your Free Time

According to researcher Mihaly Csikszentmihalyi in his book "Flow", Sunday at noon is the "unhappiest hour in America" since that's the time people are the least productive. According to his studies, individuals are significantly more motivated and concentrated at work because of the structure employment gives, and he advocates managing your spare time.

That can seem counterintuitive: shouldn't your free time be, well, free?

if you're following along at home) believes that when we don't plan our time, we either waste it on meaningless items or merely ruminate without any care or concentration. Structuring your time—even your leisure time—is shown to make you more motivated, focused, and ultimately, happy, since it offers you a direction and a purpose.

It's entirely contradictory, but when you have a reason behind your activities, you will feel much more productive and happy (even if that goal is to do nothing for an hour or two!)

3. Keep a Time Diary to See What You're Doing Wrong

Keeping a time diary of how precisely you spend your time throughout the day is one of the most effective strategies to uncover how you can better manage your time. Keeping a time diary:

Allows you to observe patterns and trends (favorable or otherwise) in how you spend your time
Lets you understand what activities affect your productivity the most (e.g. if obtaining a good night's sleep impacts your motivation the following day)
Makes you second-guess yourself when you want to spend your time on low-leverage items
Lets you assess if how you spend your time fits up with your priorities (e.g. if you consider family essential, yet spend every night watching TV) (e.g. if you consider family important, but spend every night watching TV)
When you maintain a time diary, it's a lot simpler to make adjustments to how you spend your time, because you can see, right in front of you, precisely what changes you need to do to how you spend your time. When I monitor my time, I make it as easy as possible to lessen the mental friction I have to tracking my time. In front of me, during a week, I have a notebook that tracks: what I'm doing, when I

start/stopped an activity, and any observations I have.

Keeping a diary of exactly how you spend your time seems simple on the surface, but produces profound results when you do it.

4. Do Less

Apple is one of the biggest and most successful corporations in the world for one key reason: they produce just four primary product lines. Apple manufactures the iPod, iPhone, iPad, and Mac (with software to support them), and that's pretty much all. Apple is a $431 billion firm that concentrates all of its weight on four modest product lines.

Taking a similar approach to your life is also tremendously powerful. When you do fewer things, you divide your time across less, and therefore you have far more of yourself to contribute to everything you do. I believe one of the greatest ways to enhance your attention, become a better person, and spend your time better is to do less.

Question the parts of your life, and continuously question yourself whether you're doing too much. Doing less may seem like a paradoxical method to better spend your time, but it enhances your attention and success since you can pour so much more of yourself into the things you want to achieve.

5. Think About What Matters Most to You

Everyone spends their time differently: one person may devote a lot of time to having a great job, while another may care more about putting their time into building a good family life.

Take the time to think about what you really, genuinely care the most about, then spend your time on what you care about. This sounds like basic advice, but barely anybody implements it. A lot of individuals fly their way through each day, without thinking about whether how they're spending their time will yield significant outcomes.

I believe the best way to make sure you get the most out of your time is to start with what means the most to you, then move back to your actions to find out how you should behave.

6. Focus on High-Leverage Activities

You may have heard of the 80/20 rule, which claims that 80% of your outcomes come from 20% of your efforts. I enjoy looking at the 80/20 rule in a new way: every action you perform is either high or low leverage. The more leverage activity is, the more you'll gain out of a modest quantity of work.

Some individuals put their time into low-leverage pursuits, which they receive virtually nothing out of. Take watching TV, for example. If you watch 3 hours of TV a day (the average is more than 4) and you live until you're 80, you'll spend 10 years of your life watching TV! That's time you'll never get back, and time you might have spent on a far higher leverage activity, like reading a book, having a coffee with someone you want to learn from, exercising, writing, or meditating.

When you spend your time in high-leverage activities, you can remove the cruft from your life and make sure that you invest your time in the activities that yield the biggest returns on your time.

7. Know How Little Time You Have, And Live Accordingly

This may seem like a cheesy tip, but it isn't. You don't have that much time.

If you're typical (I know you're not, but bear with me), according to the American Time Use Survey, each work day you'll spend:

7.6 hours sleeping, 8.8 hours working, 1.1 hours eating, and 1.1 hours doing chores around the house, leaving you with about five and a half hours left over for doing what you want to do.

And these figures don't include investing time into your relationships, caring for others, or any other commitments you have already.

You start every day with 24 hours, but once you subtract all of the commitments from that, you're not left with much. When you constantly remind yourself how little time you have, you light a fire under yourself to make the most out of your time. You start to say "no" to commitments that don't mean much to you. You bring more energy and drive to your work. You become more defensive of your free time and make the most of it.

Knowing just how little time you have will let you put the time you do have to much better use.

Plan Your Time Better, Use Your Time Wisely

Constantly remind yourself that you only have limited time — 24 hours a day, about 30 days a month, and 365 days a year. Make what you do every minute count so you will not waste any time doing things that don't matter.

Chapter 1

Value of time

DECISION MAKING

Not all uses of time are equal, and this basic principle may make a tremendous impact on life. People who spend their time performing more lucrative employment earn more money. People who spend their time investing in others establish greater connections. People who invest their effort in developing a flexible profession have greater flexibility. People who spend their time working on high-impact initiatives give more to society. Whether you desire more riches, more relationships, more freedom, or more influence, it all boils down to how you spend and value your time.

If you're like me, you probably desire the things stated above (friendship, freedom, effect) and others too (health) (health). But you can't have everything at once, so you need to learn how to properly handle the compromises that you confront on a day-to-day basis.

This article shows how to find out what your time is worth and use that knowledge to spend your time more efficiently. Understanding how to get the most out of your time begins with knowing—in concrete terms—what your time is worth.

The Value of Time: What is One Hour Worth?

A few weeks before I started writing this post, I was looking for a tiny travel bag. After considerable browsing I discovered one that I loved and, at only $19, it was quite reasonable. But there was one problem: the bag was created by a firm in the United Kingdom and it cost $45 to send to the United States.

I was instantly put off by the prospect of spending $45 to ship a $19 bag, so I looked for retail retailers. The firm has a physical office in New York City and I was already planning to visit the city a few weeks later. I checked the store location and calculated that it would take me around one hour to travel out of my way and stop by the store on my trip.

That's when I thought of the question that triggered this whole article: “Was one hour of my time worth $45?”
Should I save time and spend $45 to have the bag mailed to me? Or should I save dollars and invest one hour of my time traveling to pick it up in person? I had no clue whether traveling to the shop or paying more for delivery was a better use of my time and money.

The Time vs. Money Dilemma
At some level, we all have an internal barometer for how much our time is worth. For example, if someone offers to pay you $0.07 for one hour of labor, you would quickly deny it. Meanwhile, if someone offered to pay you $7,000 for one hour of labor, you would quickly agree.

On the extreme ends of the spectrum, it is simple to judge whether an activity is worth your time. As you get toward the center of the time-value continuum, however, it becomes less evident whether a given work is worth your time or not. And here is the problem: most of life is lived in the gray zone of the time-value spectrum.

For example:

Should you book the nonstop trip and save two hours or obtain the flight with a layover and save $90?
Should you pay a neighborhood teenager $20 to mow your lawn so you have an extra hour free on the weekend?
Should you spend this week working with a customer who will pay you $2,000 right immediately or working on a business concept that may earn $20,000 over the next year?
We make choices like this constantly, but most individuals base their selections on gut emotions or guesses and never assess what their time is truly worth. Everyone has an hourly value, but very few people can tell you what that amount is. Until recently, I was no exception.

How to Calculate What Your Time Is Worth
My time vs. money conundrum motivated me to seek out every expert I could find on the topic. I spoke to entrepreneurs, productivity experts, executive coaches, and even professional poker

players about the best techniques to assess how much my time was worth and how to make better choices based on that knowledge.

Then, I recorded every hour I spent over three months and estimated the worth of each hour using six different formulae. Don't worry. I've simplified all of this study and testing into a really basic approach, which I'll describe right now.

Step 1: How to Track Your Time

The first step is to quantify the whole amount of time you devote to making money, not simply the hours you are physically at work. For example, if you spend one hour traveling to work each day and eight hours at work, then it costs you nine hours to make money that day. Similarly, you should include any time you spend working on a side business or dropping your kids off at daycare. Using these figures, we are attempting to generate a full picture of the entire amount of time you devote each year to making money.

If you struggle to come up with an estimate for your time, you're not alone. Most individuals just have a faint concept of where their 24 hours go each day. If you're unclear about how much time you spend working, I propose using 2,500 hours per year as a starting point.

Here's why:

Let’s imagine you spend 10 hours every day either at work, traveling to work, or performing things linked to work. With a five-day workweek, that’s 50 hours each week. And if you work 50 weeks per year (2 weeks off for vacation), then that’s 2,500 hours per year. I'll leave it to you to make modifications depending on your unique circumstances, but for most full-time workers or entrepreneurs, I believe 2,500 hours will get you in the correct ballpark.

Tracking Time: How I Did It

As an internet entrepreneur, I spend most of my time working on the computer. When I began measuring my time, I installed a software package called RescueTime. RescueTime tracks the precise amount of time I spend on each task: how much time I spend reading each webpage, using each software application, exploring social media, and so on.

After I gathered three months' worth of data, I aggregated figures from other programs to smooth up my projections. For example, I tallied up all of my listening time on Audible to determine how much time I spent "reading" books.

Using the figures from RescueTime and a few plausible estimations, I calculated that I spend roughly 2,742 hours working every year.

Because of RescueTime's category-by-category breakdown, I was also able to organize my time into particular categories like writing, reading, website design, marketing, and so on. This extensive dissection isn't essential, but it will come in helpful throughout Part II of this essay. For now, all you need is a decent estimate of the overall number of hours you spend to generate money each year.

Step 2: How to Track How Much Money You Earn

The second aspect you need to know is how much money you made throughout the period you spent working.

This is straightforward. If you're an hourly worker or a salaried employee, simply look at your recent paycheck and multiply it by the number of paychecks you get every year. If your wage hasn't changed significantly this year, you may also look at your tax return from the previous year and simply utilize that figure. You should also include money from side hustles and freelance work since the time you spend on such activities is included in Step 1.

The figure we are attempting to compute is your take-home pay. This is the amount of money you have left after subtracting taxes. For most jobs, taxes are deducted from your paycheck, so your take-home pay is roughly what you are paid. If you are a company owner, however, you should subtract taxes and business expenditures from your top-line income.

Tracking Money: How I Did It

I use a tool called Bench Accounting to monitor my company's profits and costs. A bench is an online accounting tool that automatically takes the data from my company accounts and then a bookkeeper puts everything into tax-ready financial statements. With a few clicks, I can check how much money I've made throughout the previous month, quarter, or year.

If you are also an entrepreneur, I suggest utilizing annual revenues for these calculations since small company income may change (often considerably) from month to month. Looking at your profits over a longer time helps to smooth out these anomalies and offers a more fair value for your time.

Step 3: Calculate the Value of Your Time

Finally, divide your total money made (Step 2) by your entire time spent (Step 1). (Step 1).

For example, let's suppose you spend 2,500 hours per year making money:

If you earn $12,316/year, your time is worth $4.93/hour. This is the 2014 poverty level for a person in the United States.
If you earn $46,226/year, your time is worth $18.49/hour. This is the 2014 median income for women in the United States.
If you earn $62,455/year, your time is worth $24.98/hour. This is the 2014 median income for males in the United States.
If you earn $100,000/year, your time is worth $40.00/hour.
If you earn $1,000,000/year, your time is worth $400.00/hour.
Again, all of these estimates imply that you are working 2,500 hours per year. The figures will vary if you work more hours or fewer hours.

Are These Numbers Accurate?
When I originally computed these statistics I was startled. The worth of an hour of my time was significantly lower than what I expected it would be.

Think about how many freelancers charge $40/hour, yet don't earn $100,000 each year. Or consider how many consultants charge

$400/hour but don't make $1,000,000 per year. How can this be? The answer is these people are only being paid $40/hour or $400/hour for some of their hours, not all of their hours. When we divide their total income by the total time spent working, the value of each hour is much less than what they charge for a given hour of work with a client.

Furthermore, although we might know what we would charge per hour, we rarely calculate how much time goes into earning money outside of our working hours. By accounting for all of the time we invest to earn money, we get a clearer picture of what our time is worth—and it is usually much less than what you would charge for an hour of work on your job.

Now, if you're like me, you'd like to verify the accuracy of this first calculation. There are a few quick ways to check to see if your hourly value is accurate. Let's cover them now.

Checks and Balances

The method we just used to calculate the value of time is called the Take-Home Pay Method because it is based on your take-home pay. There are two other types of Realized Income Methods that we can use to check the accuracy of your Take-Home Pay Method. I'll explain them briefly below, but I think the easiest way to understand them is to look at the examples in Step 3 of the Time-Value Spreadsheet.

Market Rate Method – The Market Rate Method is the first way to check your numbers. The Market Rate Method is the rate you could expect to earn if you were hired by another company for a job you were qualified to perform. For example, I spend a lot of my time writing, so I could be hired for a Content Creator position. I also spend time growing the business, so I could probably be hired for a Business Development role. I looked up the salary for each role I was qualified for and then divided it by the number of hours I work to get another estimate for the value of my time. You can think of this method as what your time is worth on the job market.

Cost-Based Method – The Cost-Based Method is another way to verify your numbers.

The Cost-Based Method is the rate you would pay someone else to do the work that you do. In other words, imagine you are the boss and you have to hire someone to do your job. I started by dividing my job into specific tasks (writing, marketing, etc.) and estimating the amount of time I spent on each task. Then, I plugged in what I would be willing to pay someone to do that task full-time. Then, I calculated a weighted average of all of the tasks to come up with an overall rate that I would be willing to pay someone to do the work that I do each day. Finally, I divided what I was willing to pay by the total number of hours worked.

Once I have numbers for all three methods, I calculate the average value of my time. I figure that I might be estimating high for one method or low for another, but the value of time is probably accurate when we take the average across all three methods. Again, you can see each method in the Time-Value Spreadsheet.

How to Use This Information

We have now completed Part I. With the calculations above, we were able to determine a quick and accurate estimate of what your time is worth. Now we can narrow the zone of uncertainty and make better decisions.

For example:

If you know your time is worth $25 per hour, then you should never wait in line for 30 minutes to get a $10 gift card.
If you know your time is worth $60 per hour, then you should always pay $49 for shipping instead of spending one-hour shopping at the store.
If you know your time is worth $80 per hour, then you should always buy the direct flight that saves you two hours even if it costs $150 more than the flight with a stopover.
Once you know, in dollars and cents, how much an hour of your time is truly worth you can make better decisions daily.

At this point, we know your time is worth at least the number you calculated in Part I because Realized Income Methods only account for the income you have already earned. Ready to see if your time is worth more? Let's dive into Part II.

Part II: Expected Value Methods
This brings us to the second way to calculate the value of your time: Expected Value Methods. These calculations are based on the value you expect a given hour of work to create in the long run.

Expected Value Methods can help you make big, strategic decisions about where to spend your time. What projects should your business focus on this year? Which uses of time aren't effective and should be eliminated from your daily work routine? Should you start a business that could pay off big time in ten years, but won't make any money right away or work a stable job with a reliable income? What is the best way to manage these tradeoffs?

Let's start with the simplest type of Expected Value Method.

The Growth Multiple Method

There is a simple way to account for the expected value of your decisions. Take your net income from the previous year and multiply it by a reasonable growth multiple.

The key, of course, is selecting a reasonable growth multiple. For example, my business doubled from last year to this year, so I chose 2x as the growth multiple. With this method, we are essentially saying, "Your actions from this year will continue to drive growth over the next 12 months, so the true value of your time is higher than your realized income indicates today."

The Growth Multiple Method is an easy way to estimate how the work you are doing today will pay off in the long run, but it doesn't tell you anything about how to use your time more effectively. For that, we need to use the full Expected Value Method.

The Expected Value Method

The Expected Value Method is the final, and most difficult, way to calculate the value of time. I'm going to try to explain this in the simplest way possible, but I think the easiest way to understand it is to look at the calculations in Step 4 of the Time-Value Spreadsheet.

Here's the basic logic:

Start by breaking your time out by the task. The more detailed you can be about each use of time, the better you can distinguish which areas drive the most value.

Find a unit of measurement that connects the tasks you work on with the income you earn. For most business owners, this means you need to know the value of a "lead" in your business. In my particular case, I use email subscribers because I know the average lifetime value of a new email subscriber and most of my tasks can be linked to getting more email subscribers in some way.

Estimate the value of each task. Let's say I spend one hour working on a task that results in 50 new email subscribers. If the lifetime value of each subscriber is $1, then the expected value of that task is $50/hour. Repeat this type of expected value estimate for every task you work on.

Add all of the expected values together to determine the total expected value of your time.

Add extra variables as desired. Expected Value Methods can be as complex as you want to make them. You can account for factors like how much happiness a particular task brings to your life or how likely it is for this hour of work to continue to pay off years from now.

Expected Value calculations are highly individualized and you'll probably have to wrestle with the equations for a while to get them to work for you. Again, I think it's easiest to see this worked out in the numerical form. You can see all of the factors involved in this calculation in Step 4 of the Time-Value Spreadsheet.

Additional Notes

There are a lot of extra thoughts that go on behind the scenes of these calculations. Here are some additional factors I keep in mind when considering the value of time.

Misguided Success – Don't waste your time becoming successful at the wrong thing. Simply understanding the value of your time is helpful, but you need to know what you want out of life to get the most accurate idea of the value of your time. Too many people chase money or power or approval because everyone around them does the same. What if that's not what you want? Sure, you can find ways to increase the value of your time, but what if you'd rather have more free time than more cash? This is where knowing your core values, doing an Integrity Report, and getting clear about what is most important to you is useful.

Tradeoffs and Opportunistic Addition – Bill Gates has been named the richest person in the world more than a dozen times. In 2015, he ranked number one yet again with an estimated net worth of $72.7 billion. According to one analyst, "With a worth of $72 billion, a 6% rate of return would earn Gates roughly $114.16 per second he is alive, making it a poor investment for Bill Gates to bother picking up a $100 bill if he dropped it."

Although interesting and quotable, the idea that it isn't worth it for Gates to bend down and pick up a $100 bill off the ground is incorrect. Why? Because picking up the $100 bill does not prevent Gates from earning $114.16 at the same time. He will be paid whether he picks up the $100 bill or not. In fact, by picking up $100 Gates will earn $214.16 during that particular second instead of his normal $114.16.

Picking up a $100 bill is not a tradeoff that prevents Bill Gates from earning money. It is an opportunistic addition on top of the money he is already earning. Opportunistic Addition refers to choices that would decrease the value of your time if you spent all of your time on them, but increase the value of your time if you do them at opportunistic moments. For example, consider an author who also does speaking engagements. If they spent all of their time speaking, then they would decrease the value of their time because they wouldn't write any new books, they would gradually become irrelevant and their speaking rate would decrease. However, by doing speaking engagements now and then—say, once or twice per month—many authors can add thousands of dollars to their bottom line while still having plenty of time to write new books.

Non-Negotiable Free Time – One of the dangers of calculating the value of time is that you end up convincing yourself to work another "productive" hour so that you'll increase the overall value of your time. According to an article in the Wall Street Journal, "Some researchers say assigning an economic value to time risks harming people's quality of life. Those who are encouraged to focus solely on the dollar value of time tend to feel impatient and pressured, says Jeffrey Pfeffer, a professor of organizational behavior at the Stanford Graduate School of Business. They work more and spend less time in rewarding activities such as volunteering or enjoying music."

For my part, I decided that I would track my free time to see how many hours I was using for leisure vs. work, but I wasn't going to place a dollar value on that time. Instead, I elected to say that my free time was non-negotiable. Having free hours where I could relax and decompress made it possible for me to be effective during the working hours that remained. You need to value your free time, downtime, and leisurely activities that provide whole health and wellness to your life.

Should you work another hour? I – Wondering if you should work another hour? Here's a good rule-of-thumb I learned from Sebastian Marshall: Consider each hour of your day. 9AM to 10AM, 10AM to 11AM, and so on. On average, do you make net positive or net negative decisions during that hour? For example, if you work late, does the hour between 9 PM and 10 PM lead to positive outcomes on average? Or does that hour include more mistakes than accomplishments? Does that hour include more procrastination than productivity? If it's a net negative hour on average, then you should stop working. Working hard on a project is good until the next hour of work burns you out more than it produces something valuable.

Happiness and Meaning – If you want, you can account for factors like how much happiness or meaning a task adds to your life. However, rather than build these variables into my actual equation, I decided to rank them for each task from 1 to 10 based on how fulfilling it was for me. I didn't use these rankings in any equations, but they can act as a tiebreaker between tasks that are close in Expected Value.

Where to Go From Here

Calculating the true value of time is much harder than it sounds and far more powerful than it seems.

The value of your time will likely change every year, perhaps even faster. The methods I have laid out in this article are flexible and adaptable. As you spend more time in a particular area or earn more income, you can simply plug the new numbers into the spreadsheet and get an updated value of your time.

Chapter 2

Time is money

We hear "time is money" so frequently that we forget what it means. When we say "time is money" we typically imply that people who save time will save money. "Time is money" because labor requires time. But if time = money, those who hold money on other people's time. Right?

Indeed, as workers, we agree to contribute our labor and time in exchange for money. We contribute our time, and in exchange, we receive a specific amount of money. Time equals money implies that saved money is saved time, acquired money is gained time and lost money is wasted time. Let's create a timely example...

How much time did you lose today?

By buying Bitcoin, individuals have invested their saved time in exchange for electronic confidence. The more individuals spent their saved time, the greater the value of Bitcoin as it gathered the time from its investors.

For those who invested early, one day of their time mysteriously became 19 days. As individuals began selling their Bitcoin, the Bitcoin body started to lose time. As a result, the saved time of those who bought late began to lose value. If you purchased bitcoin at 19,000 and sold it today, you lost half of the time you spent. Someone else now owns your time. Why? Because they performed better than you. How is it possible?

Value

Here is the trick: Not everybody's time has the same market worth. The greater your performance, the more you gain every time unit. The money you have in your wallet symbolizes not simply the time you worked, but also the market worth of your time. Your time is less valuable if your job doesn't collect other people's time. The more time from other people you can acquire with your time, the greater your performance.

If time = money, then those who possess money on other people's time. Jeff Bezos, the wealthiest man in the World, possesses $110,000,000,000. The typical American makes $60,154 per year. If time equals money, then Jeff Bezos owns 1,828,639 years of the typical American's life. In Somalia, he'd possess 200,000,000 whole human years. That is if money equals time. Is there no escape from that terrible logic?

Quality

Saving money short term might squander time long term. In the long run, low quality is costly. A molded Ikea chair may seem good and cost a fraction of an original Eames chair, but chances are that it fails in a few years and you need to purchase a new one. Eventually, you lose money purchasing substandard quality. In the end, you squandered money and, as we now realize, that means you wasted time.

Investing time might save money if you invest it in quality. This is a frequent justification for marketing handmade items, brands, and premium stuff. "It's more costly, but you will own it much longer! " Unfortunately, not everything that is more costly will last longer. Sometimes you simply pay for the brand. Sometimes a product is purposefully more costly to fool you into thinking it is of greater quality. Often it's a combination. It's important to spend your time before you spend money. Attention and care may save time.

Using attention and care to identify quality also applies to time itself. The quality time you spend with people you care about, at home and work, doesn't transfer into Dollars.

Don't be tricked. Not everything is countable, weighable, or quantifiable. Not everything converts into money. In the end, your life is not measured in Dollars spent or saved, but in years spent wisely. No matter how much you make, no matter how well you do compare to Jeff Bezos, the most important thing you have is your time. Time is money, but not like 1+1=2.

Knowledge is power. Power doesn't equal wisdom.

The Top 7 Ways You Are Wasting Your Time

If you discover it takes you far longer to finish tasks or meet deadlines than your co-workers, you need to assess how you are using your time and determine how you might become more efficient. You are holding yourself back if you do not think about how you can better manage your time, and how you may improve upon time squandering behaviors. If you are not sure where and when you are squandering time, here are a few frequent ways you may be wasting your time:

Being Disorganized

If you are spending time attempting to locate documents and people, not focusing on priority tasks first, and generally find yourself continuously trying to keep up with your colleagues, then you are unorganized, consequently squandering a lot of your time. Spend time arranging your desk, and start prioritizing your work so you are on the same page with your colleagues. Invest some time now in being organized, then always waste time playing catch up.

Procrastinating

Wasting time because you do not want to accomplish something when you might have already done the work with the time you've squandered is time you will never get back. Procrastinating is quite prevalent, yet such a disadvantage to development and efficiency. Whether it's because you just do not want to accomplish anything or because you are terrified, become someone quick to confront their worries and grind through their task. The sooner you begin the sooner you will be completed, and you will create a habit of getting all things done effectively.

Reading The News

It is so easy to be caught up in the 24/7 news cycle, and with all of the investigations and issues of this administration, the cycle seems bottomless. The news seems more like a reality tv show these days, and it is simple to not stop watching. To control the time you spend reading the news, do not be drawn in. If you are on deadline, do not make the newest controversy the reason you miss it, there will be another scandal to follow so concentrate on your job.

Scrolling Through Social Media

The simplest and most prevalent method to squander time is social networking. If you find yourself looking at your phone or checking your accounts when you have a tough moment or want to find a way to procrastinate, put your phone away so it is a chore to get it and consider getting software that blocks social media sites like "Freedom" and "self-control." If you need to take a break, find a productive, rejuvenating break, like a walk for some fresh air and a cup of tea instead of looking at social media.

Gossiping

Talking about other people does nothing for you. You will not be better at your job or a better colleague if you talk about others. Spend your time more effectively, and virtually any other activity is more productive than gossip.

Worrying

Worrying is a waste of excellent energy. If you are concerned about something, take action so you do not worry about it. If it is out of your control, then leave it alone and concentrate on other things. It is just not constructive to merely sit and fret about things, and use that energy somewhere.

Checking Email

You may spend the bulk of your day replying, sending, and monitoring emails. Designate particular periods of your day for reading and composing emails, and leave your email alone outside those hours unless it is critical.

Chapter 3

How to manage your time

A Brief Guide to Time Management

Time management is the process of planning and controlling how much time to spend on specific activities. Good time management enables an individual to complete more in a shorter period, lowers stress, and leads to career success.

Benefits of Time Management

The ability to manage your time properly is vital. Good time management leads to better efficiency and production, less stress, and more success in life. Here are some benefits of managing time effectively:

1. Stress relief

Making and following a task schedule reduces anxiety. As you check off items on your "to-do" list, you can see that you are making tangible progress. This helps you prevent feeling stressed out with anxiety about whether you're getting things done.

2. More time
Good time management gives you extra time to spend in your daily life. People who can time-manage effectively enjoy having more time to spend on hobbies or other personal pursuits.

3. More opportunities
Managing time well leads to more opportunities and less time wasted on trivial activities. Good time management skills are key qualities that employers look for. The capacity to prioritize and schedule work is immensely valuable for any business.

4. Ability to realize goals
Individuals who practice good time management can better achieve goals and objectives and do so in a shorter length of time.

List of Tips for Effective Time Management

After considering the benefits of time management, let's look at some ways to manage time effectively:

time management tips infographic

1. Set goals correctly
Set goals that are achievable and measurable. Use the SMART technique for creating objectives. In essence, make sure the goals you set are Specific, Measurable, Attainable, Relevant, and Timely.

2. Prioritize wisely
Prioritize tasks based on importance and urgency. For example, look at your daily tasks and determine which are:

Important and urgent: Do these tasks right away.
Important but not urgent: Decide when to accomplish these chores.
Urgent but not important: Delegate these responsibilities if feasible.
Not urgent and not important: Set these aside to do later.

3. Set a time limit to complete a task

Setting time constraints for completing tasks helps you be more focused and efficient. Making the small extra effort to decide on how much time you need to allot for each task can also help you recognize potential problems before they arise. That way you can make plans for dealing with them.

For example, assume you need to write up five reviews in time for a meeting. However, you realize that you'll only be able to get four of them done in the time remaining before the meeting. If you become aware of this fact well in advance, you may be able to easily delegate writing up one of the reviews to someone else. However, if you hadn't bothered to do a time check on your tasks beforehand, you might have ended up not realizing your time problem until just an hour before the meeting. At that point, it might be considerably more difficult to find someone to delegate one of the reviews to, and more difficult for them to fit the task into their day, too.

4. Take a break between tasks

When doing a lot of tasks without a break, it is harder to stay focused and motivated. Allow some downtime between tasks to clear your head and refresh yourself. Consider grabbing a brief nap, going for a short walk, or meditating.

5. Organize yourself

Utilize your calendar for more long-term time management. Write down the deadlines for projects, or for activities that are part of finishing the entire project. Think about which days might be best to dedicate to specific tasks. For example, you might need to plan a meeting to discuss cash flow on a day when you know the company CFO is available.

6. Remove non-essential tasks/activities

It is important to remove excess activities or tasks. Determine what is significant and what deserves your time. Removing non-essential tasks/activities frees up more of your time to be spent on genuinely important things.

7. Plan ahead

Make sure you start every day with a clear idea of what you need to do – what needs to get done THAT DAY. Consider making it a habit to, at the end of each workday, go ahead and write out your "to-do" list for the next workday. That way you can hit the ground running the next morning.

Implications of Poor Time Management

Let's also consider the consequences of poor time management.

1. Poor workflow

The inability to plan and stick to goals means poor efficiency. For example, if there are several important tasks to complete, an effective plan would be to complete related tasks together or sequentially. However, if you don't plan, you could end up having to jump back and forth or backtrack, in doing your work. That translates to reduced efficiency and lower productivity.

2. Wasted time

Poor time management results in wasted time. For example, by talking to friends on social media while doing an assignment, you are distracting yourself and wasting time.

3. Loss of control

By not knowing what the next task is, you suffer from a loss of control of your life. That can contribute to higher stress levels and anxiety.

4. Poor quality of work

Poor time management typically makes the quality of your work suffer. For example, having to rush to complete tasks at the last minute usually compromises quality.

5. Poor reputation

If clients or your employer cannot rely on you to complete tasks promptly, their expectations and perceptions of you are adversely affected. If a client cannot rely on you to get something done on time, they will likely take their business elsewhere.

Conclusion

In conclusion, time management is a very important skill to be learned and to be mastered to have a better lifestyle. By managing time well, you will no longer suffer from stress, and your work/tasks will be done on time and with great quality. Remember that it is important to have the attitude to change your schedules and to change procrastination. Also, take into account all of the explained strategies that are very helpful to achieve better time management. It is important to add that sports also provide a helpful hand for time management, and also permit your body to be healthy and to have a better social circle. I hope you have enjoyed this web page, and that it has helped you to achieve better time management.

I hope that the strategy I've shared here will remain useful for you as time goes on.

www.ingramcontent.com/pod-product-compliance
Lightning Source LLC
LaVergne TN
LVHW020606160826
845677LV00020B/3866